A CHILD'S GARDEN OF MISINFORMATION

Books by Art Linkletter

People Are Funny
Kids Say the Darndest Things
The Secret World of Kids
Confessions of a Happy Man
Kids *Still* Say the Darndest Things
Kids Sure Rite Funny
A Child's Garden of Misinformation

A Child's Garden of Misinformation

LOVINGLY HARVESTED BY

ART LINKLETTER

Illustrated by Charles Saxon

PUBLISHED BY   BERNARD GEIS ASSOCIATES
DISTRIBUTED BY RANDOM HOUSE

© 1965 by Bernard Geis Associates

All rights reserved under International and Pan American Conventions. Published by Bernard Geis Associates; distributed by Random House, Incorporated, in New York and simultaneously in Canada by Random House of Canada, Limited.

Library of Congress Catalog Card Number: 65–16511

Manufactured in the United States of America

Third Printing

Portions of this book were previously published in *McCall's* Magazine.

157288

To Michael Arthur, Dennis Jack and Laura Ann Linkletter (sons and daughter of son Jack and his wife Barbara), Kevin Andrew and James Arthur Zweyer (twin sons of daughter Dawn and her husband John Zweyer), and to the many other grandchildren the future will bring, with the help of Robert, Sharon and Diane, my remaining unchained Links.

Acknowledgment

Few people have traversed the bewildering paths through *A Child's Garden of Misinformation* as expertly as Harold Dunn, the Missouri schoolteacher who helped me prove that *Kids Sure Rite Funny* (in a book coincidentally called just that) and who harvested many of the dizzy daisies that make up this new bouquet of boners. My thanks to him, and to Mrs. Barbara Warner Goldberg, whose watchful eye spotted some of the brightest wild flowers along the garden paths.

A. L.

Contents

Foreword

IN MY FIELD, lengthy introductions may be very impressive to the man making them, but to the listening audience they are usually nothing more than stage-waits. I learned early that when I have a good act to introduce, it's best to say so simply and briefly and leave the stage to the performer.

And I have a good act to introduce, a star act, a return engagement—with an all-new cast—of those kids who say and do the darndest and funniest things.

I've arranged and edited the material, aided by the same team that helped me put together the earlier books, but the kids are the stars. I'm just as much a part of their audience as you are, and I'm just as eager as you for the show to start. I'll run on stage occasionally—very occasionally—to ad-lib a few lines, but mostly I'll be sitting out there with you and laughing just as hard. It's the kids' book—and they're a joy!

ART LINKLETTER

A CHILD'S GARDEN OF MISINFORMATION

CHAPTER 1

In Daze of Yore

ONE OF THE occupational hazards of putting together *A Child's Garden of Misinformation* is that a man finds himself bursting into laughter at the strangest times and places. The thought of some kid's boner, blooper or howler comes to mind, and suddenly you're laughing out loud at the innocently funny view that kids take of a complex world—while the family looks at you strangely and wonders if Dad's off his rocker, or (much more embarrassing) a crowd of strangers looks nervously around for an attendant in a white coat.

It happened again last night. My wife Lois and I were alone in the living room when, in the middle of a sentence—*her* sentence—I remembered a definition I had added that afternoon to the history chapter of the book: "Russia was ruled from 1682–1725 by Peter the Great. His mother named him his first name and he named himself the rest."

Now, the first lesson that every husband learns (the hard way, usually) is that the most unforgivable thing he can do to his wife is to enjoy a private joke in her presence. It's a violation of the marriage vows—didn't he promise to love, honor and share all the punch lines? There's only one thing worse: for a man to talk in his sleep just loud enough for his wife to be interested but too low for her to make out any words.

"What," Lois inquired, "is so funny?"

Lois and I share a love of kids and the honest humor that springs from them, and I had hoped to surprise her with the completed book, and further hoped it would bring her as much pleasure as my first Child's Garden of Misinformation, *Kids Sure Rite Funny.* So now I explained my bootleg boners, ending with the gem from history I'd just remembered.

Feeling that I was winning my case, I offered more evidence: "The first world war started because of a difference between Adam and Eve."

Even as I said it, I felt that in the situation it wasn't the happiest choice, so I quickly offered another: "In Africa, it was either Livingstone who found Stanley or the other way around. Anyhow, they got together. One thing I'm sure of it wasn't Lewis and Clark."

Lois laughed out loud—but I had the uneasy feeling that she was laughing more at me than at what the kid had written.

"What," I asked, "is *so* funny?"

She laughed again, then answered with two words that have become a Linkletter family joke: "Freddy Martin."

Those of you who have read my story, *Confessions of a Happy Man,* know what she meant. Freddy Martin was a leading bandleader at the time I was beginning in broadcasting. Lois and I had just become engaged, and I brought her along one night so that she could hear me introduce the band coast-to-coast and appreciate how important a man she had landed.

Holding her hand I casually approached Freddy at the bandstand. "Freddy," I said (nothing like a first-name basis to impress her), "Freddy, I want you to meet Miss ———" and my mind went blank.

Both Freddy and Lois stared at me, but all I could do was stand there, get red in the face and emit a few gurgling sounds.

It is a story that Lois always delights in telling, but only on those occasions when it makes a definite point.

"Keep your perspective," she laughed. "When little Mary Smith forgets the name of Fabius Maximus, remember that *they* weren't engaged!"

I laughed at her teasing. We share the same perspective about children—our own and others. The enjoyment they bring to me never arises out of a feeling of superiority. I never laugh *at* them, but always *with* them—and also at the distant memory of a young Art Linkletter who bonered, bloopered and howlered with the best of them.

I laugh from historical experience.

As a kid, I threw a firm hammerlock on every historical fact that inadvertently crossed my path. It was a friendly rivalry, and after the encounter we would go our separate ways, neither the fact nor I ever quite the same again.

After all, how important can history look to a kid? The younger ones think that *anything* that happened before the day they were born is all a wild rumor. The older, more sophisticated kids, however, are aware of recorded history—the latest album by the Beatles, that is.

Naturally, everything eventually falls into place. The boners and bloopers are left behind as a heritage for the next class. The weeds of misinformation in a child's garden are pulled out and hardy perennials of fact are planted.

It's part of growing up, and it's inevitable.

And it's also much less fun.

"Fellow citizens," Abraham Lincoln said, "we cannot

escape history." Maybe not, Mr. Lincoln, but we're about to meet some kids who led it a merry chase. *And if you hear anything in italics, that will be me whispering in the back of the classroom.*

No humans were born during the first of the world because this was the preastork age.

Ancient was a long time ago, maybe even before that.

Thence is like Then, only much longer ago.

Descendants are those people who presently reside in the future tense.

The Christian martyrs were thrown to the lions—fathers and children, too.

B.C. and A.D. had a big battle about 2000 years ago. A.D. won and we have been on A.D. time ever since.

Well-cooked meat was rare for the cave man.

One of the best values of history is learning what little they knew.

History must have been a snap course to the kids of One Million B.C., but since then each day has added SO much of it—how can it be kept straight by a kid who has trouble keeping his own room in order? His version is Incorrect, Impossible—and, maybe, an Improvement. . . .

It may sound strange that Socrates was born in 470 and died in 399, but everybody in those days lived backwards.

When the use of fire was thought of by Early Man, what he thought of it depended on what it was doing.

Rich people of Long Ago couldn't afford beautiful printed books. The mainest reason was they weren't invented yet.

The civilizations of the Saxons and Visigoths were subsequently previous to each other.

The Tarsals and Metatarsals lived in the foot of Italy.

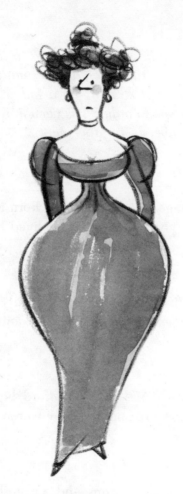

An hourglass was a lady's figure popular in Olden Days. As the lady grew older, she gradually sank to the bottom.

The early inhabitants of Istanbul thought they were living in
Constantinople. It was not for many years that the mistake
was discovered.

The Mooers got their name from worshipping sacred cows.

There's enough truth in the kids' off-center observations to remind us again that History is really just a long-running performance of People Are Funny. . . .

The King was called Henry the Ate because he was always eating.

The wars that the Romans fought against Carthage were called Puny Wars.

Many people in Babylon succumbed to Tiglath Pilesar, a fatal disease of the time.

One of the chief occupations of the Arabs in the fifteenth century was Sicily.

Athenian art was kept at Surpassing Heights instead of in the city.

Q. In what channel was the Spanish Armada defeated?
A. I think it was channel 4.

Olden sailors were often battered about by fierce unexpectant squaws.

Columbus first sighted land at page 22.

Magellan explored because he was curious. People often said, Isn't Magellan a curious person?

Magellan made the 1st trip around the world and when he returned to Spain he told how he had been killed in the Philippines.

Q. Letters to the New World were carried in Packets. What is a Packet?
A. Something a sailor puts his hands and other things in.

Disobinate sailors were put in charge of a cat with nine tails.

Trade winds are what sailors took along to bargain with the natives.

If you think the kids were in deep water when they talked about sailors, keep reading and you'll find out that they can drown on dry land, too. . . .

Diogenes spent his time wandering around with a lantern looking for the discovery of electricity.

Some Queens can't marry Kings so they arrange to have Concerts.

Minnesingers traveled from town to town. They didn't really sing too good, which is the main reason they kept moving.

Egypt was started in the NE corner of Africa a long time ago and has occupied the same location to the present time, but sometimes under different management.

Following the Hapsburg line, Austria was next ruled by the line of Demarcation.

The Doge's Palace was another name for the Royal Kennels.

The Sulphate of Magnesia ruled the ancient kingdom of Epsom.

A connoisewer was a member of the French underground.

A Phoebus was an ancient Greek mode of transportation.

The countries that had serfs were called futile systems.

When the Roman Army was defeated, General Upheaval took over the government. He did this several times.

Tutonic People means people who are 2-tone, like white skin and black hair.

The Baroque Period means when Bernard Baroque was active.

The Baroque Period means like this—. . . . . instead of the ordinary period we use today like this—.

The two-party system began when the big people sat at one table and put all the kids by themself.

After a hard day fighting a knight would send his armor to the museum for the class to visit with the teacher and then pick it up the next morning.

The discovery of gunpowder changed the face of the world because it exploded in everybody's face at the slightest excuse.

New York was discovered by Explorers of Old who recognized the tall buildings.

Colonial expansion was caused by constant overeating.

World War Two was fought all over the world and other places.

Other places? That leads naturally to our next chapter, which is filled with observations on Space by youngsters who are probably the first generation of kids who will really be "out of this world." We adults may think of Space as merely a place we can never find when we want to park the family car, but kids KNOW. Here's a teaser:

The Rocket Development Program is to find more dancers for the Music Hall.

Eyes right—and BLAST OFF!

CHAPTER 2

How High Is Up?

$\mathbf{M}$Y GRANDCHILDREN, when they grow old enough to voice
an opinion (which, among Linkletters, occurs very early),
probably won't be able to grasp the fact that their grandpop
lived in a time when the only thing a man could do with the
moon was to sit under it with his girl.

They may laugh and write me off as incurably square when
I stroke my beard and tell them that one of the big moments
in my life was when I, as a teenager, stayed awake with the
rest of the world for nearly every one of the thirty-three
hours it took Lindy to cross *merely* an ocean.

And they *won't* laugh when I try to defend my generation
of scholars by telling them that a great many of us went to
school and *majored* in Space: The Taking Up Of.

To the kids of today, racing for the moon is a prosaic fact;
to me, it still sounds like an old theme song by Vaughan
Monroe. They're all Space-age babies—and the incredible

21

facts of that new era come naturally to them. It's a little disconcerting to their earthbound, lost-in-the-stars parents.

I've looked over some of their test papers, and I want to reassure my confused, adult world that Space—that mysterious world we grew up to know as the Great Unknown—is, in the extremely agile brains and capable, reaching hands of some of our youngsters, *still* the Great Unknown.

Of course, they're entitled to a few unmanned space slips before getting into orbit. In the meantime, it's comforting to know that over in the little red schoolhouses in Russia, some Ivans and Katrinkas are probably writing exactly the same answers.

There's never a Space lag in kids' boners. . . .

The best influence the moon has had on the earth so far has been to stay out of our way.

When the moon is between the sun and the earth, we have a lunatic eclipse.

Q. On some clear nights we do not see the moon. Why not?
A. Because of invisable clouds.

They took a lot of pictures of everything on the moon except its backside.

When we send two men to the moon it will be called the
Jimminy Project.

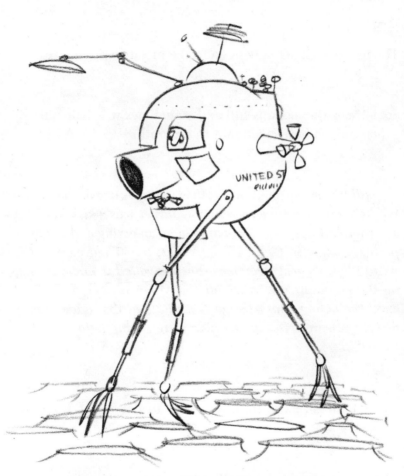

We know much more than anchant peoples did. They
thought it was 240,000 miles to the moon. We found out
it was 240,000 miles. The difference is we *Know*.

Some people say the moon is made of green cheese which
seems like spending a lot of money and going an awfully
long way to get something I'm not too fond of in the first
place.

The first person actually to go to the moon was a monkey.

Sometimes the moon is full and sometimes it is half full depending on how much rain that month.

*I still like my generation's rather limited view of the moon.
We had our Countdowns—but the target was a kiss. We also
went into orbit, and if astronauts have an eating and sleeping
problem while in flight, we had that, too. They may call it
Astro-Physiological Reactions, but we called it Love. It may
be the mightiest use to which the Moon is ever put, and I
envy the young who become test pilots in that adventurous
field of research. But as the kids were saying before I inter-
rupted . . .*

It is 93 million miles from the earth to the sun as the crow
flies.

Astronomy is to look in the sky and see stars while astrology
is to look up and see lions and virgins and other spooky
creatures.

It will not be as bad coming back from the moon. It is down-hill all the way.

The big ones in the sky are called Stars and the little ones are Starlets.

Some of the planets have rings and some are single.

The Big Dipper is the father of the Little Dipper.

Anyone interested in the weather might ask how clouds are made. I am not going to say for sure until I find out the answer.

When sunlight hits the air around earth it gets the bends and turns all sorts of colors.

The sun is really a star. How it fools us is by shining in the day and being of the unpointed kind.

Q. How far is it from the earth to the sun?
A. First think how fast it takes light to travel from the earth to the sun. Now think what the speed of light is. Figure the numbers together. Now you have guessed it right.

Sometimes we bawl the sun out for being so hot. But without the sun to help it, a tree could never make shade.

If you see a martin, don't shoot! It is not from Mars. It is just a bird.

The two most important things a navigator should remember are where he is and where he wants to go.

Meteors are stars that are so hot they have to leave in a hurry.

The Milky Way was discovered by Louis Pasteur.

You can always find directions from the North Star unless it's cloudy, in which case Tough Luck.

Air is called Atmosphere when we want it to sound more important.

Solar Energy is energy you use when you fly by yourself.

A Light Year is when there's not too much homework.

Rockets get their energy from either solid or liquid fools.

Because it has plant life, Mars is called a Plant.

Venus moves from 10 to 20 males an hour.
(*I think the rate is higher in California.*)

It takes the earth 24 hours to roll over.
(*I KNOW this happens faster in California.*)

For zillions of years there was a sun but no earth. This kept man from making much progress.

The earth has been here a long, long time. But the sun has been there a long, long, long time.

Pluto can be seen with the naked eye at Disneyland.

Cyclones are caused by hot and cold running air.

O-zone is right next to P-zone.

Night and Day and Seasons are just a few of the advantages of belonging to this Solar System.

Stratus fear is something astronauts get, but they take a pill for it.

The sky is like a wall to wall ceiling.

And how would you parents like to pay for that at 11¢ a square foot? As you noticed, I didn't have too much to say while the kids were flying around—it's an attitude that grownups often display when a youngster's reaching for knowledge goes beyond the adult's grasp. Some label it Patient Understanding, but I call it by its right name: Chicken! Anyway, I'll be back on solid ground in the next chapter on Grammar and Punctuation. That's my subject. You may al-

ready know that I almost became an English teacher. Back at San Diego State they still remember the state champion-ships I won in two of the most gruelling events—Splitting the Infinitive and Dangling the Participle. I have twice been elected president of a national organization dedicated to Stamping out the Semicolon. If there's anybody; who can, handle a chapter! on Grammar and Punctuation: it's me?

Or is it I:

CHAPTER 3

How to Puncture
a Sentence

I THINK I'VE always been under the spell of language, ever since I learned as a youngster that syntax was not the name of the offering I put into the church collection plate each Sunday morning.

Written or spoken, language has always meant to me the power of communication, and that was important to me even long before radio and television came into my life. To know what I wanted to say, and to say it as well and clearly as I could, has always been my goal. I knew it might be the mysterious ingredient that spelled the difference between getting ahead or getting lost in the shuffle.

Maybe it began at my birth in Moose Jaw, so named, historians tell us, because it was a place where "man mended his cart with the jaw of a moose," whatever that means. Anyhow, I've been mending the various "carts" in my life ever since with the jaw of a Linkletter (more numerous than

31

moose these days, if only for the reason that fewer hunters are taking shots at us).

As I grew up in San Pedro and San Diego, this urge to communicate helped me to convince customers to buy papers from me, girls to take a summer evening's walk with me, sceptical employers to give me a needed job, and the world in general to accept the minority opinion (held by me) that Art Linkletter was a man to watch.

Yes, a man has to communicate. And, unless you're Marcel Marceau or Elizabeth Taylor, for most of us that means words and grammar and punctuation, three sharp tools that can shape a future.

But, like any tools, you'd better learn to handle them carefully, or you'll botch up the job.

Come along with me and meet a batch of young botchers. They'll grow out of it, of course, but for this chapter at least the sign over the door leading into the classroom reads: "English Spoken Here??"

Oh, yes—in Kids Sure Rite Funny! *one kid wrote that "Italics are what the Italians write in"—but here, again, it will only be me whispering in class. . . .*

Some words are directly objectionable to a verb.

A period is used after a true statement. If it's a lie, use an exclamation point.

Nouns have different sexes but you don't know until you look at their genders.

A period is to let the writer know he has finished his thought and he should stop there if he will only take the hint.

The object of a verb is to get things started happening.

! and ? and : are all useful for puncturing a sentence.

Commas are used when you have to take a breath, and periods are used when, you want to stop and think. . . .

I know I should never end a sentence with a preposition so I'm not going to.

With that basic refresher course, you should be ready to rush ahead to English II—and even if you're not ready, it won't (as one kid wrote) make "a participle of difference."

Past Tense means you used to be nervous.

Whom is an uppitty form of Who.

A which is a pronoun except on holloween.

Hyphens connect the parts of a word and are very rarely found by themselves.

Grammar is what the teachers learn us.

"She" is a relative pronoun only when you are talking about your mother or aunt or niece or somebody like that.

A vowel is something two people take before they marry.

Demonstrative adjectives are adjectives describing monsters.

Parenthetical expressions are things mothers and fathers are always saying to each other.

A confound sentence is one that somebody has stuck a comma in.

The future tense of the verb "to marry" is divorce.

The past tense of think is thawed.

The Greeks, so they tell us, had a word for it. Kids, too, have a word for it—and even if it's not the right one, you can be sure it's an unreasonable facsimile. . . .

Watchwords are words you can see as they are spoken. We have no watchwords in English.

Racoon can also be spelled raccoon. There should be more freedom of spelling like this. For when a word is ruled by one spelling, it destroys initiative.

A paradox is what adults tell. When a kid does it, it's called a big lie.

Disinterested and uninterested are words that have different meanings and you have to be careful not to get your dis and your un mixed up.

Before you decide between using the words Bring or Take,
find out if you're coming or going.

Proper English is when you say gender instead of sex.

Semantics is the study of monkeys.

Adored is the past intense of love.

Anachronisms are happenings in the past imperfect tense.

There is a big difference between m and n. Take the word "acme." With three loops you are at the top, but with two loops you only have pimples.

A foreign language would be bark bark to a cat.

The present tense means right NOW! No, it is too late. That present is the past tense now. You have to look fast to catch the present.

Quatrains are used to get from one poem to another.

The fact that people and trees and elephants and cars all have trunks just proves that there are more things than there are words. Avawaca, keompsri, eeps. If everyone else would give three new words the shortage would soon be helped.

You should never capitalize the word Yucca unless it is the first word in a sentence.

If you see "octopi" you are looking at them plurally. If you see an "octopuss" you are looking at something singular.

English was called Anglo before it came to this country.

We shouldn't use the word Alright, but if you write it like "all right" then it's perfectly alright.

A pentameter is a lion with five feet.

Vice Verse means a verse that makes as much sense backwards.

To be verbose means to use so many words in what is said that you don't need them all to get the thought across if it was to be said without being too wordy or verbose.

Good spelling comes much easier when words are properly prounced.

Author! Author! One of the best ways to learn is to go to the great writers and see how they do it. It should help, unless . . .

Robert Frost got a Pullet Surprise for his work.

Henry Wadsworth Longfellow was one of our best known and beloved pots.

The climax of his African adventures is reached when the author is set upon by an unfriendly tribe of wild sausages.

A book not based on fact is called fiction. A book based on fact is called faction.

In writing a story, Mark Twain always did a twist at the end.

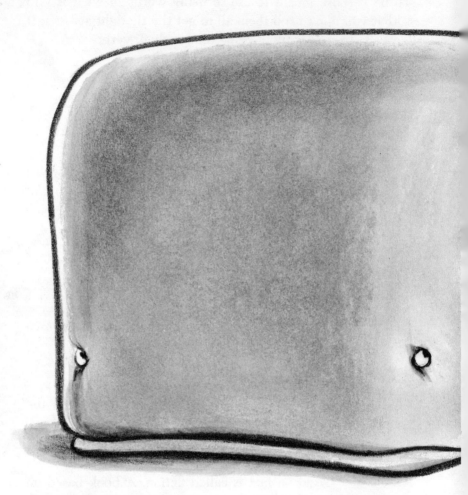

One of the favorite sea stories of all literature tells about a
sea captain that is mad at a whale for eating his leg. He is
filled with hatred as he mopes around all through the book.
He gets the name of Mopy Dick.

Good writers avoid cliches like the plague.

Any questions? Of course, but this time it's the teacher asking and the kids answering, and if the questions and answers don't seem to match up, don't stifle the kids' initiative—after all, they may grow up to be doctors who develop cures for no known diseases. . . .

Q. Use the word "warrant" in a sentence.
A. I wouldn't be learning English if it warrant for you.

Q. What is a synonym of the word "sear"?
A. Roebuck.

Q. What is the difference between Pot and Pod?
A. Pod is the way you say Pot if you talk with your mouth full.

Q. What mistake did I make in this sentence: "It was me who volunteered to work for him."
A. You should never volunteer.

Q. Can you use the words "back" and "front" in a sentence?
A. Boys I am around a lot I am not backward in front of.

Q. What is the difference between the words "lose" and "loose"?

A. If some money falls from a man's pocket, lose is what the money is to the man and loose is what it is to the pocket.

Q. What is an adverb?

A. I was sure sick the week we studied adverbs.

Q. Use the present and past tense of "sang" in sentences.

A. He sang in the mud. He sung to the bottom.

If you think the kids took you down the garden path in English, wait until you romp with them into the next chapter where they're let loose in a real garden. If you find a green thumb in the crowd, it's only because they've been carrying around lime drops. Come on, pardner, let's head 'em off at the Mulch. . . .

CHAPTER 4

Why Plants Get Potted

THE OBVIOUS REASON why plants get potted is that they want to forget their troubles—and one of their biggest troubles seems to be the misinformation that each generation brings to its first contact with them.

What self-respecting plant could survive a session with these hobbledehoy horticulturists and not scream for something stronger than water?

I had a normal upbringing as far as flowers and trees are concerned: trees are for climbing and carving initials in; flowers are those magical things that always seem to patch up a quarrel with your girl friend.

Of course, I'm not entirely uninformed on the subject. Lois and I always have lovely flowers in and around the house, and I enjoy and appreciate them. I know that when two gardeners are discussing an American Rose, they don't mean Billy; and if a girl says she spent the afternoon gathering phlox, she's not necessarily Little Bo-Peep.

But there are so many trees and so many flowers, and young minds haven't had the time to sort out all the names and vital statistics, even if they have the same desire to know that drew Francie Nolan toward her one tree in Brooklyn. That never stops them, however, any more than it used to stop me. And as we all proudly display our "green mind," the results can sound like Luther Burbank with amnesia.

There is seldom such a thing as a boy tree or a girl tree, even the Mable tree has a neuter gender.

When a farmer takes the twig of one plant and ties it onto the twig of another, this is called grafting or corrupting.

Erosion is when the ground has dry scalp.

Some wine is made by stomping on grapes. This kind of wine is called squash.

Moisture finds its way to the tree through the tree's routes.

An apiary is a place where they grow apes.

A tundra is a vast treeless forest.

A tamarind is a tropical fruit. We eat the tama and throw away the rind.

Eggplants are where baby chicks think they came from.

Saplings are trees that don't know any better.

A perennial is a flower that continues to live after it dies.

A prune is a plum that didn't take care of itself.

Sarsaparilla is easier to find than it is to spell.

One of the by-products of rubber is the rubber tree.

Plantetariums are places for planting plants.

Seaweeds is something you don't want your neighbors to do when they look in your garden.

If you eat a toadstool and don't die it's a mushroom.

Self-pollination is a tree that is its own father.

In winter most trees get bald.

Grass seed gives us grass, but don't expect the same results with bird seed.

The sunflower is in the same family as the dandelion but they hardly notice each other.

If you look at a maple leaf and it has parallel veins it isn't a maple leaf.

Potted plants will drink practically anything.

You is an evergreen tree, not to be confused with Yew, which is a female sheep.

Rushes are plants that you need in a hurry.

The walnut tree is famous for both its wood and its nuts, but you can't have your wood and eat it too.

Very few people have actually heard a birch bark.

Q. What is made from the eucalyptus?
A. Eukeleles.

Q. During hot dry weather, all trees in the forest are in danger of a common enemy. What enemy?
A. Stray dogs.

Dusting a crop is not like dusting a house. When you dust a crop you make everything dustier than before.

A hybrid is a thing that is not its real self.

Chlorophyll is something plants have to make them smell nice to other plants.

A corn borer is an insect which severely radishes the corn crop.

Q. Where are the seeds of the poppy located?
A. At any reliable seed store.

Olives are delicious unless you can't stand their taste.

Pussy willows are another name for cat-tails.

Plants live on the carbon dioxide we breathe out. If you want to kill weeds, don't breathe in their direction.

Growing from bulbs we have such things as onions and lights.

The sugar tree is sometimes called the maple tree, being named after its type of sugar.

Rhubarb is a plant that angries people.

Dwarf plants were developed by Mendel, who first lowered the bloom.

CHAPTER 5

Health in a Jocular Vein

Eᴀʀʟʏ ᴛᴏ ʙᴇᴅ and early to rise may make a man healthy, wealthy and wise, but some of the kids I meet today seem to be following their own poetical advice:

Up until midnight, sleep until noon,
If things get too tough we'll go to the moon.

While still here on earth, however, a kid has a difficult time keeping the eternal verities clearly in view. There is always the decisive crossroad decision: Early to Bed or Watch the Late Show. And if it's the Late Show, which it usually is (have you seen the latest ratings?—Early to Bed isn't even in the first fifty), he gets further instructions on how to be *really* healthy, wealthy and wise.

An aspirin has a drag race with another pill down to the trouble zone; tired blood goes to bed early while its owner goes out dancing; the most popular boy in class got lousy marks but had 22.7% less cavities. To your health, sir!

The kids have an advantage over the rest of us, despite the flow of misinformation that surrounds them. They're younger than we are, and have more time to get the picture in perspective. But until they get things straightened out, some of their answers will send the A.M.A. to bed.

Take the one a little girl gave me when I asked her what she did to keep her good health and sound body. "A sound body," she said, "is when a kid carries his transistor radio around."

Maybe you should read this chapter in bed—IF you retire early and get up at the crack of dawn. . . .

Two good sources of starch are potatoes and collars.

Clavical is a medical condition commonly known as having a collar bone.

Playing with knifes is one bad cause of strip throwts.

Although we sometimes try to cure a ham, it usually stays dead.

Premeditation is what you do before the doctor comes.

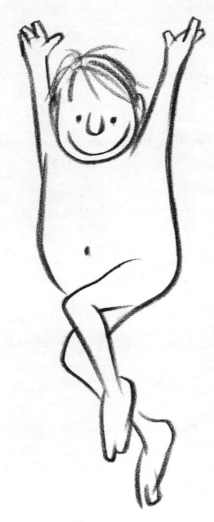

Here are four tests for aliveness—Do you eat? Do you grow and change? Do you use oxygen? Do you move? If you answered yes, yes, yes and yes, you are alive.

Prognoses is the medical term for the study of noses.

If you hit a man in the jocular vein it can be fatal.

An epicure is something that wipes out epidemics.

Swollen rivers are caused by infectious germs in the water.

Lungbago is a disease of the lungs.

Anyone suffering from electrical shock should be put in an insulation ward.

Insurgents are doctors for the rebel side.

Most people have an attack of physique at least once in their lives.

If a man is drowning you should give him mouth-to-mouth recitation.

Q. Will you get warts if you handle a toad?
A. This is a fact that seldom comes true.

Pasteurized milk comes from cows which graze in pasteurs.

The Mnemonic Plague is remembered to this day.

Bury Bury is usually a fatal disease.

An antidote is a medicine you take to prevent dotes.

Q. What should you do for hives?
A. Nothing. They are enemies.

Every epidemic is followed by a hypodemic.

Celibacy is how you feel after too much celebration.

People should not eat on a full stomach.

The future tense of diseased is deceased.

The Salt Vacine can be obtained by all members of the Immunity.

Chicken pops come from petting you know what.

In eating too much for Thanksgiving, the fun is not afterwards.

※

Consumption is a disease in which the person eats hisself up.

※

Miasma is a physical condition in Florida.

※

Obstetriks is a disease my mother catches every year.

※

Sinus is a polite word for hole in the head.

※

Some thermometers are filled with mercy.

※

The first thing a doctor does in an operation is to make an excursion.

※

Polo has been wiped out by vaccination.

※

98.6 is the normal temptation of the body.

※

Radium was discovered by Madman Curry.

Skin is like wax paper that holds everything in without dripping.

Not being long-nosed, humans use the word Trunk to describe someplace else of them.

I have been intoxicated against polio.

Women usually live several years longer than people.

The brain sits in the seat of consciousness.

Gymnastics exercise your outsides while Genetics exercise your insides.

A snore is a breath that talks.

Immure means to stick someone in jail. Immune means to do it with a needle.

Doctors know hypodemics can never be fatal if they are shot in the arms or other non-fatal places.

Quack doctors are for curing lame ducks.

A minute is a very short time unless you are holding your breath.

The worst thing about my trip were the long hang-overs between planes.

As for birth control, I am against it for humans but for it against insects.

Upheaval means you shouldn't have ate so much.

When your face turns red from over-coughing is what is meant by the expression hoarse of a different color.

If a lady is a carrier of a certain disease she is called a Typhoon Mary.

Chlorofarm is a place in the country where animals go to sleep.

Yogi is how you get from drinking too much yogurt.

Much has been said about vitamins so I won't add anything.

We all need well-rounded meals. Square meals cause indigestion.

Waiter, the check, please. We're in a hurry—some very important discoveries are waiting for us in the next chapter. . . .

CHAPTER 6

Fission + Fusion = Confusion

THE BASIC FACT that I've grasped about Fission and Fusion is that everything in nature is either breaking apart or coming together all the time. I've felt that way myself on too many occasions. It's comforting to know that all of life is just an endless series of Big Nights and Mornings After. If we can continue to keep together or break apart the proper items and not get them confused, I guess we'll make it through the week.

Sometimes the scientists have to lend a pretty big hand to get the processes moving. It takes time, and that's where the trouble begins. Maybe we should take science out of the hands of the scientists and put it in the firm, capable hands of the kids. No one is as expert at breaking things as they are, and they are acknowledged masters at bringing together unique combinations that no one else would think possible.

You can test my theory in this chapter, as the kids ap-

proach all scientific matters with a clear eye and open mind
—and a rugged defiance of all natural law.

(Note to scientists reading this book: Laugh along with
the rest of us—but, please, stay on the job, huh?)

Cold makes everything get smaller and Heat makes everything get bigger—if you forget about ice cubes.

Vacuums are nothing. We only mention them to let them
know we know they're there.

A fact was only a theory as a child.

Gravity means a person can't fly. And Nature can get pretty
stubborn about it.

Friction is everywhere. Don't move unless it is absolutely
necessary. There is a little friction in all of us.

Chemistry was begun by alchemists who were looking for
gold but had to settle for chemistry.

Every snowflake is made into a different shape. Is this all
scientists have to find out?

Nitrogen is a nun burning gas.

Humidity is the experience of looking for air and finding water.

Sleet is rain or snow that cannot make up its mind which.

Meteorologists do not really get paid for studying meteors. What they do get paid for I don't know.

Tornados are usually accompanied by high winds.

The speed limit for gales is 75 miles. After and above that they get called hurricanes and other names.

Although I weigh 88 pounds, I weigh only 40 kilograms. Everybody weighs less in the metrical system.

Heavy water is like with ships in it.

The general law of accelerated bodies is that the faster a body goes the quicker he gets there.

The most ice-free season is salt.

Proclivity is a natural tendency. There is a man standing on the edge of a cliff. There is a strong wind. The rest is proclivity.

If you see lightning no you don't. You see electricity.

As of yet, we know only how to make compasses pointing in a single direction.

When your thermometer says "100 degrees," cross your fingers and hope it is speaking in fairenheit.

The more a humidity goes over 100% the harder it rains.

Q. When a glass is dropped, what causes it to break?
A. Carelessness.

When wind stops blowing it is just air. When wind starts blowing again it is March.

A watt is called that until we can find out what it is.

The top of a room's air is hotter than its bottom.

Before a 1000 ton ship will float someone has to misplace 1000 tons of water. This is the captain's job.

A.M. radios can be listened to only in the mornings. I think F.M. radios means you can listen on Friday Morning.

Gravity is with us most in the fall.

Well water is water that won't make you sick.

Specific gravity is the direction of straight down.

When a gun is fired, if you don't see the smoke before you hear the noise, you're dead.

This damp weather is hard on my science.

My experimental materials are a box of matches, a candle and an empty glass of water.

Voltage tells the age of electricity.

Milk is pasteurized at a temperament of 165 digress.

Molecules move. It is true! (When we are not looking, of course.)

The way to get a magnet to work is to mark it with an N.

Q. What are the three dimensions of matter?
A. Interior, exterior and ulterior.

Q. If you put the tip of a thermometer in boiling water, what would it say?
A. Take me out, if it could talk.

A weather vane tells the direction of the wind. When the wind blows in various directions, use a varicose vane.

It is a well-known rule that opposites attract. That is why magnets work and boys marry girls.

Here is how to prove there are molecules. First look at a whole pile of sand. Next look at each separate grain of sand. Now that we have proved that we can go on to another experiment.

If a portable radio is turned in different directions, the station talks loudest behind its back.

Thunder is the noise that air makes when lightning jumps through it. So would anybody.

Bodies of water come from the Dead Sea.

Thunder does all the barking but it's lightning that bites.

Fog is a low, lying cloud. When it is around, you might as well not mind looking at it.

Just think of what God can make from something when He made this whole world from nothing.

And just think of what the kids will accomplish when, in the midst of the fission and fusion and confusion, they have a foundation like that to stand on. It can move mountains and cover the earth, which just happens to be the subject of the next chapter of boners. Let's see how fast the kids move and what they cover. . . .

CHAPTER 7

Rocks, Ridges
and Red Hot Java

ONE OF MY earliest boyhood memories goes back to the time we were living in a rickety little house at Point Fermin, near San Pedro on the southern California coast.

Just beyond the house there were some cliffs that looked out over the sea. They were only about a hundred feet high, but to a child's eyes they seemed as impressive as the Matterhorn.

I had to climb them.

And I did, one day, crawling out on the highest ledge to get an exciting view of the waves crashing against the rocks below, sending towers of mist almost as high as the ledge on which I sprawled.

When I started back, the way was impassable, made wet and slippery and uneven by the mist and leaping waves. I was trapped, and I remained trapped until just before dark, when someone heard my cries and brought the San Pedro fire department to the rescue.

That experience should have ended my desire to climb, but it didn't. I've climbed many cliffs and mountains since then, in many places, although I still don't completely understand why. I know the classic answer, "because it's there," but I think it's just the natural curiosity of a boy or a man to know everything he can about the mysteries surrounding him. A back alley in a quiet neighborhood or old Mr. Johnson's pasture across the country road can be just as much of a challenge to a kid.

That's why I think I understand what was in the mind of each child as he wrote the sentences you'll read in the following pages. Children are curious about the big place in which they live, but mountain climbers and explorers, like poets, must always make sure that their grasp is firm, even though they want to leap far beyond. Otherwise, they may find themselves trapped on a mental ledge called a Boner, without the San Pedro fire department around to rescue them. It's something to laugh about—after it's over. Let's join them in the laugh.

Oh yes—I eventually DID climb the Matterhorn—in Disneyland. . . .

There is a tremendous weight pressing down on the center of the earth because of so much population stomping around up here these days.

Soil is helpful dirt.

Rock is what you call everything you don't know the exact name for.

The main use of Oil today is to get people rich.

Altho geologists know that it is very hot at the center of the earth, they do not know exactly how hot. Only bad people know for sure.

Sand is found in both hot deserts and cool seashores. It can grow anywhere.

Metallurgy is the study of how to keep people from being allergic to metals.

Gilt is gold that is stolen.

When geologists see loose rocks on the ground they know this is a good sign. So, they get set to start digging. They dig and dig and the lower they dig the closer they know they are coming to It. And then finally, there It is—SOLID ROCK! That's how they make a living.

The ocean stores its excess water on its continental shelf.

It now appears pretty sure that Maine is slowly sinking. When we first noticed this we fought Spain, thinking they were causing the sinking of Maine, but that wasn't it.

The importance of geology to geography is that, without geology, geography would have no place to put itself.

Geologists are interested in the earth's beneath.

Water can be gotten from rocks! The magic word to say is
Porous, like in porous a drink.

Q. What is the modern geological era called?
A. The modern geological era.

Rocks are gradually softened through aging. The first hundred years of a rock's life are the hardest.

Manganese is named that because it was discovered together by the Mongolians and the Japanese.

Eb and Flo are the names of the Tides.

Q. How did the Paleozoic Era end?
A. Very slowly.

Anytime I see sedimentary rocks, I stop and think how things had to be squished together to make it for me to see.

We can call crude oil "crude" if we want to, but just don't ever forget how much we depend on it.

Volcanoes give us hot java.

Coal is a product that more and more we need less and less of it.

People find gold in fields, veins, river beds and pockets. Whichever, it takes work to get it out.

Diamonds are found on the backs of diamondback rattlesnakes. That is why they cost so much.

If you pour acid on metal you can get itchings.

Another name for magnesium silicate is talc. We call it talc because who would want to put magnesium silicate on a little baby?

Limestone is a green-tasting rock.

Erosion is caused by rose water.

Streams are for more than just running and holding fish. They are also for wearing down rocks. And swimming.

The natural enemy of rocks is wind, water and weather, which are always trying to cut it down to size.

When a landslide is in slow motion, you better not be.

If a volcano dies you may call it extinct. But you must not call a dead animal extinct until all his relatives are equally dead.

Oil is formed by the process of waiting.

Q: How has man wasted the earth's natural resources?
A: By taking coal and burning it.

Earthquakes are caused by horizontal up and down movements, giving an unsteadying effect to everything.

Copper ore is spelled o-r-e so no one will try to row with it.

When we cover a can with tin we say it is tin plated. Don't say pleated. *Plated*. Pleating is what sheep do.

Fossils are dug up by archologists. If dogs dug them up we'd call them bones.

Now that we've dug the earth in all its improbable wonder, let's sneak a slightly foggy peek at its chief inhabitant,
Man. That's you and me, in case you don't recognize the
subject of the eager research ahead. . . .

CHAPTER 8

All About Anato-Me

As a father five times over and now a grandfather, I've had a great deal of experience, and enjoyment, in watching a youngster literally discover himself.

It's a big moment, greater than Balboa seeing the Pacific for the first time, when a baby finds out that those wiggly things on the ends of his arms can be useful in picking up all kinds of interesting objects, and that the ones on the ends of his legs can have other uses besides putting them in his mouth—standing on them, for example. There are so many pieces of interesting equipment: Nose, Ears, Belly Button, Teeth, and all the Etceteras that make up the human anatomy—and they all belong to *him*.

It's a fascination he will probably never lose for the rest of his (or especially *her*) life, even when he takes daily inventory from the top of his thinning hair to the corn on his big toe.

Kids have more fun doing it than anybody—it's like turning a new census taker loose in an uncharted territory. Some of the facts and figures he unearths may not be accurate, but they're funny....

The four stages of man are infancy, childhood, adolescence and obsolescence.

Our inherited traits are carried in our jeans.

The temporal bone holds the temper in place.

Laps are so that more than one person can sit on a chair at a time.

Heretics is what you get from your father and mother.

It is important to take careful care of our bodies, for where would we be without them?

The particles that tell what a person will be like are Gene's. Nobody knows his last name.

The nonstrils are the part of the nose that isn't there.

The humorous vein supplies blood to the funny bone.

A scarlet is a little scar.

An octupus is a man who fits glasses to your face.

Your waste is between you and your bottom.

The brain (usually located in the head) does not tell us to breathe. What tells us is the Instinct, which nobody knows where it is located.

If a man has only one of them why is it called an abdomen instead of an abdoman?

Men can reach maturity but only women have reached maternity so far.

A nostrum is a very long nose. You can cure anything by smelling it with a nostrum.

The saliva glance is when you can tell at a glance if a person is alive.

Everybody has a thyroid gland which helps the body burn up food, so why do we cook it in the first place?

Appendixs are useless things that every body still has left over from some surplus body.

If you look at a person's farhead you can tell how far he will go.

Nowadays everything is specialized. The brain specializes in thinking and the muscles specialize in working. It used to be different somehow.

Trunks are for storing valuables in, so the human trunk contains such valuables as stomachs, hearts and a lot of other stuff.

The sternum is the bone we sit on.

The patella is the knee. Water on the knee is called flotilla.

The iris is the pleasant part of the eye, like in iris eyes are smiling.

Sounds are vibrations of our vice box.

There are cavities all through our bodies. That is all right as long as they don't get into our teeth.

The saliva glands are sometimes also called pitui glands.

Everybody is either a man or a woman. Nobody is neutral.

Veins could very well be called something else if it were not for the lack of a better name.

Metabolism is a way of changing matter into energy without having to mess around with atoms.

Without red cells, blood would bleed to death.

The way to remember a body cell from a prison cell is that they are in people instead of people in them.

To waist away means to go on a diet.

In our study of anatomy last year I was Chairman of the Hind Bone Section.

A mutation is a change of body while a transmutation is a change of trains.

The three races of man are The Kentucky Derby, Belmont and The Preakness.

The biceps and triceps are in the arm, but forceps are usually found in the mouth.

The body has more cells in adulthood than in any of the other hoods.

Skin is used to hold people in. It is the original corsit.

To upbraid somebody means to fix their hair.

When you breathe in you inhale and when you breathe out you expectorate.

For some strange reason I feel like singing I Ain't Got No Body. *If you've reassembled all your stray parts, put your best foot forward to the next chapter. The kids have done a pretty good job on Man—let's see what they do to the Machine. . . .*

CHAPTER 9

Unpopular Mechanics

THERE'S A SCHOOL of thought which believes that the crucial battle of our time will be Men *vs.* Machines. Automation already has a big foot in the door. No one quite knows whether we own our automobiles and television sets or they own us. Scientists are predicting that the human anatomy will dwindle away to a puny figure with only one giant finger capable of pushing buttons. Machines are already announcing the results of elections when 99 per cent of the people have not yet voted.

Fortunately, there are some statistics on our side. Most importantly, our population has risen to almost 200 million— and no sociologist has yet claimed that the machine was responsible for *that!*

So, I suppose, the battle of Men *vs.* Machines is still undecided, and the balance of power is in the hands of the next generation, some of whom have contributed to this chapter evidences of their own little struggles with the world of machines.

Let's see how they—and we—are doing. . . .

A finished product is one that has already seen its better days.

The block and tackle are two positions in football.

A treadmill is where they make tire treads.

In cars there are two kinds of brakes: lucky ones and un-
lucky ones. I'm not sure about the difference but my
daddy has one kind and my mother has the other kind.

An internal combustion engine is one that explodes when started.

Raw material is before you cook it.

The thing that goes up and down on a machine is called a lover.

The first trains had to be pulled by steaming Injuns.

Hydro-electric damns are what you'd hear if a man stepped in a puddle while using an electric shaver.

Last week I thought how to invent a screwdriver except it had already been thought of.

Mechanical answers are easier for me to understand than mechanical questions.

Before man could build an elevator, he first needed to find a tall building.

Water wheels are wheels made of water. They are to be looked forward to in the future.

The bit was a bit when it bit into the wood. Also, it only took a small, that is a bit of, a bite. That was a second good reason for naming the bit "the bit."

I found out how the wheel-and-axle works by removing a doorknob. I both found out and got in trouble.

The U.S. Treasury Dept. uses big stamping presses to help stamp out coins. If they had their way I guess we would only use paper money.

Hubbub is the sound of a hub needing oil.

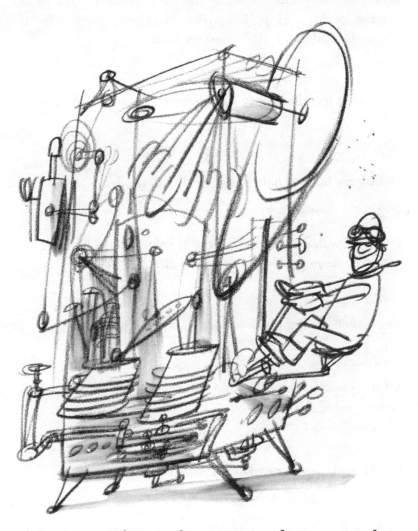

If you can teach a machine to go without moving from there, you have taught it how to vibrate.

When we blow into a whistle, the air is pushed together in some places and pulled apart in others. Nacherally it screams and that is the sound we hear.

My watch has the ability to run on either standard or daylight time.

Dames are built to hold water until it is needed.

Plenty of water in the radiator will keep it from blowing its top. Some in the driver will help also.

The wheelbase is a place you go to if you have a flat.

A fixed pulley is an irresistible resistance wrapped around an immovable axis.

Honky-tonks is what early cars were called.

Air brakes are very good, but I'm not sure if they work when the car windows are closed.

A dynamo is an extinct animal.

What made the wheel so important as an invention is that it didn't just roll. It could also travel.

Turbines are ladies hats worn by men in some eastern countries.

The book said that paper is made from wood or rags that are chopped up and pounded into a wet pulp similar to cooked oatmeal. I tasted it, and somebody's lying.

Don't look now, but I think the Machines are slightly ahead. In fact, this entire chapter has been a recorded message. Now, if you'll press the third button from the top, the page will turn, and we'll plunge into the next gulf of misinformation. . . .

CHAPTER 10

Everything From H to O

W<small>ATER FASCINATES KIDS</small>. They run toward it, and they run away from it. They love it in a lake or an ocean, but it's a necessary evil in a bathtub. They'll swim in it, sail on it, dangle feet in it—but fight to keep it away from that sacred area behind their ears. They'll delight in getting their fingers sticky with soda-*water* and *water*melon—then fight to the death any effort to apply just plain soap and water to those same fingers.

It's kids-ophrenic!

But they *are* fascinated with it, in most of its shapes and forms, as you well know if you've ever watched a small tot pick it up in his hand, squeeze it, and then stand mystified as it eludes him. He likes to look at it, touch it, taste it, smell it, and listen to its changing voices—sometimes a roar, sometimes a whisper.

And as they grow kids learn more about where water

comes from, where it goes, what it does, how it changes—
but there's so much water, and so many facts about it, that
a young brain can get water-logged. When that happens, a
fact can sink before it's fairly launched.

So all aboard while the S.S. *Misinformation* embarks on
its short though adventurous cruise. Some kids are taking
that trip in this chapter, and just so they (and you) will
know that others have sailed these waters before, let me con-
fess now that it took me too many years to discover that the
Bay of Fundi was *really* larger than the Bey of Tunis.

Cast off. . . .

Water is 100 proof humidity.

Water cannot be split into any smaller particle than the
common drop.

When ice and water are put in the same glass the ice always
  comes to the top. One of them has to, and it would look
  kind of silly the other way.

In making water, it takes everything from H to O.

A mixture of oil and water is called an emotion.

For fish wishing to eat as well as drink, ocheans are highly flavored with salt.

Rain is huddled and snuggled vapor.

Water is a longer abbreviation for the word H2O.

Three states of water are the Colorado, the Missouri and the Mississippi.

Evaporation gets blamed for many things people forget to put the top on.

When you mix water and air you get humility.

Q. What happens to the ice in a glass of water?
A. The water eats it.

If you think those comments don't hold water, let's take a few side trips and find out if the kids are in their element with the other elements . . .

Talking about whether gas expands when it is heated, I would definitely say yes and no.

Alkaline can cause red litmus paper to turn blue. So far as I know, this is its only talent.

Synthesisis are useful for the purpose of holding chemistry together.

Glycerin is a sweet oily BOOM!

Say you have some nitrogen. That is alright. Say you mixed it with glycerin. Then don't say I didn't warn you.

Sound waves are now used to ferment wines. These sound waves are very high.

Hot weather makes the mercury in a thermometer struggle up and up and up. It would rather just sit there and be cold.

A fire must have oxygen, but not too much. Giving it too much is known as blowing it out.

Hydrogen is a bombious gas.

Iron is very useful unless it meets oxygen. Then it is rust. It is like a person getting in with the wrong crowd.

Philters were magic things put on cigarettes a 1000 years ago. Of course, there were no cigarettes of that long ago, which is what made the philters magic.

One of the more useful by-products of fire is heat.

If you put a piece of copper in a hot flame, fine powder starts forming on it. This is the way copper says Ouch.

One thing to remember about mixing acids is don't.

Only 21% of the air is oxygen. Every time we burn a fire it takes oxygen. Don't start fires for the sake of our remaining oxygen.

Fire and combustion are much alike, except fire burns things down while combustion burns them up.

We have found many answers to many unknown problems about chemistry. Now the thing is to find out what problems these answers fit.

Molecules are made of atoms. Atoms are made of energy. Energy is made from wheaties.

Molecules all pull toward each other. They have learned the value of sticking together. Because of this, even though they are very tiny, molecules will probably never become extinct.

Nothing would be anything without molecules.

Now that we know how to get energy from atoms, the next big break-through is to figure out how to stuff our excess energy back into atoms.

The best thing carbon monoxide is good for is running away from.

Oxygen can be burnt. Engines know how to do it.

Q. Iron has a higher melting point than glass. Why?
A. Because you just said so.

When a liquid is heated it is changed to a gas. When a liquid
is cooled it is changed to a solid. If you drink it right away,
you don't have to worry about those other problems.

Encyclopedias are good places to get information on carbon,
unless you don't really want to know that much about it.

Hot water rises to the top. Even if it changes to steam and
becomes air, it will keep going up. The only thing that can
stop this process is a ceiling.

And back to water for two of my favorites—one showing the poetic turn of our kids' minds, and the other the practical side....

Sugar disappears when it is dropped into water because it is not sanforized and therefore shrinks to nothing.

Dew is air that looks wet.

And as the S.S. Misinformation *slowly sinks into the sunset, we turn our attention (and page) to the best laid plans of Mice and Men, which you can bet your last dollar will go astray in the hands of our kids. And don't hide your heads, because something new has been added....*

CHAPTER 11

Of Mice, Oschtriches and Men

Dᴵᴰ ʏᴏᴜ ᴋɴᴏᴡ that a camel can live for weeks on the food stored in his dump? Or that the most common breeding ground for the boll weevil is the Cotton Bowl? Or that a skunk is known for its unpleasant ardor? Or that you can lead a horse to drink but you can't make him water?

I didn't either until I invaded the animal kingdom created in our kids' imaginations. They bring 'em back alive, but slightly battered. If the animals aren't wild, they will be after some safari member repeats to them what the kids had to say about them. For the rest of us, however, it's just good clean fauna. And I can assure the animals that, whatever they hear, the kids really love them—you can feel it in their boners. . . .

And if you, the reader, should die from laughing while reading this chapter, be assured that all your friends will pay their respects—because, as one kid reminds us, it's an honor to be a polar bear at a funeral. . . .

Caterpillars are made of fuzz and squash.

🦖

Bats make many sounds that we can't hear, but since they're not talking to us anyhow what difference does it make?

🦖

Most mammals but man are talebearers.

🦖

Werewolfs are wolfs in the past tense.

🦖

The rarebit is a seldom seen rabit.

🦖

An octupus sleeps inside a tentacles.

🦖

Nobody knows if an octupus is waving its arms or kicking its legs.

🦖

The down on birds keeps them from flying too high.

🦖

Insects are found in many sizes, shapes and cupboards.

🦖

Alligators hatch out of eggs just like birds. They shouldn't try to be something they aren't.

Dauschounds get their unusual courage from having plenty of backbone.

Giraffes are a rich source of necks.

The boll weevil is worth millions of dollars to wool growers.

Boy cows have more horns and less milk.

If you are a girl sheep you are not a you, you are a ewe.

Sponges cannot live out of water. They are found in oceans and bathtubs.

When beavers are angry they slap the water with their tails. It helps them to take it out on something.

An octupus swims backwards. But with him nobody knows the difference.

All people with six legs are insects.

A Click Beedle can lay on his back and flip himself over. This gives him something to do.

Dinosours kept humans extinct until much later.

The remains of most dinosaurs were not found. Lucky for us some of them had the presents of mind to step into a tar pit for preservation.

When animals seem to be thinking, they are usually only instincting.

The ant-eater is also sometimes called an earth-pig, I guess by ants mostly.

The scarlet tanager has a scarlet body and a tan elsewhere.

A mumbo jumbo is an elephant that can talk.

Baby foxes grow up in four months. Baby elephants take almost twenty years. He has much higher to grow.

A dog is a man's best friend and when he licks you it is not from beating you up, it is from getting you wet.

Both tigers and zebras have striped skins, but under the skin they stop being brothers.

When a moeba wants to meet another moeba he can do it all by himself.

A Siamese Cat is two stuck together.

Tadpoles get that way from having a fish mother and a frog father.

So far as I know there are only two types of ants, red and black. And that's enough.

Monkeys and men are both primapes.

Snakes are not all bad. Some snakes are useful. One thing they are useful for is making belts.

Cocky Spaniards are a breed of dog.

A mite is an insect worth only a small amount.

Do you know there is a difference between a frog and a toad? I don't either.

The most dangerous part of killing a snake is its head.

Storks get their own babies by the egg method.

To learn the sex of a chicken, you can look at the egg and get no hint at all.

A hen usually cackles when he lays an egg. It is mostly to show off.

My fater is lerjic to cats.

Q. How do fish travel?
A. In a class.

Q. What is the difference between a mother deer and a father deer?
A. A father deer has hitlers.

If fish could be mammals, the sea horse would be the first
to do it.

Some reptiles are helpful to man by eating harmful bugs and
little animals. Some other reptiles are harmful to man by
eating him.

A horse sometimes has a lopsided gate.

A queen conch is the length of a foot. Anybody's.

All animals have either instinct or extinct.

Even when the chameleon loses his tail it does not hurt, so oh well.

Anybody wanting to be a bird is not allowed to have teeth.

Q: What are the three parts of an insect?
A: Interior, exterior and posterior.

"Gator" is what you can say if he is so close you don't have time to say "alligator."

A tock is a female tick.

Pumas are mountain lions. Little ones are called pumice.

In order to be a vertebrate, the thing that wants to be it must have a backbone. Lobsters only wear their backbones on their outsides, like somebody only thought of it at the last minute.

Insects invented antennas long before TV.

Tigers have stripes but Leopards have spats.

Anthropoids are things like gibbons, gorillas and chimpansies. And us.

They're called Whopper Cranes because they are very large.

The most common amphibians are frogs and turtles. A horse would be called an uncommon amphibian.

Grasshoppers' ears are hidden under their wings and crickets wear theirs on the front legs, so no wonder they can't hear people trying to tell them to go away.

Oschtriches stick their head in the sand to show they are stoopid.

I have a dog. His name is Mitzy. He is black with a long white back. He licks me in the ear when I come home. He thinks of me like I think of stamps.

The way an alagator looks is like he is mad at the world, even if it don't bother him.

Penquins are birds. They dont fly, but they cant fool me that way.

The stork is a highly over-rated bird. I know.

The platypus would be a mammal except he lays eggs. But that isn't too bad a thing, so I vote to let him go ahead and be one.

Butterflies are at first long worms. But then they start living right.

Sometimes before you find out if it's a bull or a cow it's too late.

Howl Bleat Roar Bark Scream! These are some sounds made by animals. Was this your first experience at hearing them all at once?

Allagators bellow to attract their mates and their mates don't make an issue of it.

Squids have suckers on their arms. You have to be a sucker to spend your whole life on a squid's arms.

Don't feel sorry for the sheep when his wool is cut from him. Since the wool is then pulled and twisted and wound, isn't it the humane thing to cut it off the sheep first?

Don't be misled by the name quarter-horse. It cost me 50¢ to ride one.

A scalawag is a dog that acts friendly for its own purposes.

Fleabotomy is the study of fleas' bottoms. There are not many men doing this work.

If any reader is encouraged by that last item to leave his own work and flee into one of the few fields that does not seem to be overcrowded, don't do it until you've perused the next chapter. After all, Politics and Government may be your game—especially as explained by our embryo electors. . . .

CHAPTER 12

Fellow Representatives and Centaurs

A LESSON THAT our country learned early and well, and which some countries unfortunately never learned or learned too late, is that each citizen had better take an active interest in running his country or he may suddenly find the country running him.

I've always admired the men and women who make the personal sacrifices required of anyone who stands for office. We can't all do it, but we *can* be as knowledgeable as possible about candidates and issues and long-range policies.

Lately (and I want no remarks about my grandfather status), I've noticed that the world and its politics seems to be getting not only smaller but also younger.

Young men and women can be found in elected offices from community level to Washington. Young people have joined in the day-by-day, door-to-door work of the party of their choice. In the last national election more people voted for a presidential candidate than ever before in our history, and the largest percentage increase shown by any group was among the young voters. Teen-agers, too, joined in, and one of the political buttons most seen wherever you went was this one: "If I were old enough, I'd vote for ————."

I find this youthful awareness attractive and delightful. This generation of kids seems to be alert to the lesson that each generation must learn for itself: Ready or not, they'll be handed the reins some day. I think they want to be ready.

The kids in this chapter haven't reached that point yet. They're still grappling with the fundamentals—and not always winning. As in everything else, there is such a profusion of facts to be absorbed that some get lost or mishandled in the rush. Their comments about government and politics may be foggy, but sometimes, in a roundabout way, they hit a great truth right on the nose.

Pull the curtain behind you and pull down the lever—it's a laugh landslide. . . .

Q. What are the qualifications needed to be a United States Senator?
A. To get more votes than the other one.

Representatives represent the people while the senators represent the states.

Senatorial courtesy means to stop calling the other senators names after the election.

Each state elects two centaurs.

A governor must be an American citizen of the country to which he belongs.

Saying what you really mean is caused by wearing Freudian slips.

The Child Labor Law abolished children. Of course it has since been repealed.

What you make is your income and what the government takes is the outcome.

Sometimes senators make speeches that are 100 pages long. It would even tire them out just to have to turn all the pages. That is what page boys are for.

An incompoop is an overworked budget.

An exofficio was an unreelected office holder. He still is for all I know.

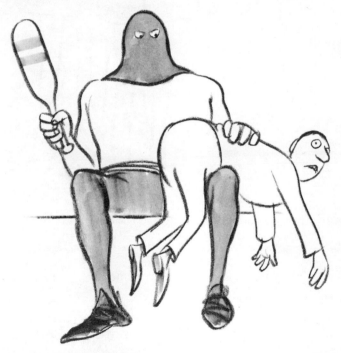

When somebody has a debt, in arrears is where it will happen if he doesn't pay up.

A quorum means enough people are there to start the quorrel.

Callus is what we should have toward none.

Committees are to get everybody together and homogenize their thinking.

A whereas is a legal document.

Factions are fights. They are located in otherwise friendly groups.

Armistice Day is when many countries signed a treaty and said that they would never fight again, but they did.

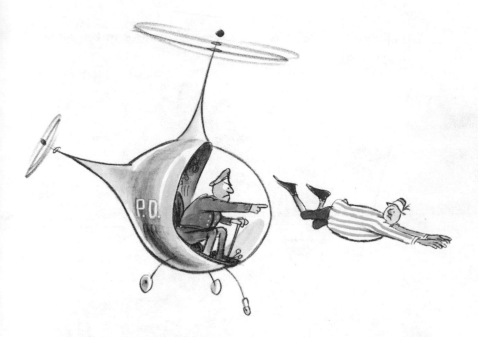

One of the first laws passed by Congress was the Law of Gravity, which was a reminder to not go flying around without an airplane.

If the government wants to change the constitution it has to do it with a mendment.

A public servant is one who serves the public for his own good.

A judge is called an umvirate. If you have three of them it's a triumvirate.

A prejudiced person is one who doesn't believe in the same things we do.

Under the American system, economy sizes are big in soap flakes and small in cars.

The three branches of government are land, sea and air.

To be conscious of an act means if it is bad you are sorry about it as soon as possible.

Even though a caste might be untouchable in India, he could be a movie star in Hollywood. It is the American way.

Bartering means say like you have some corn but no money and you want some oats, well that is as far as I understand bartering.

A net prophet tries to guess how many fish there will be.

A corp. is a dead business.

A government floats a loan by sending it to the country in a waterproof bottle.

If the government does not want a ship to leave port, they can put a lumbago on the captain.

The national gross profit is how much the government thought it made before the bills started coming in.

Rhodes scholars study our traffic problems.

An invoice is your conscience.

As a former president said: "If you can't stand the heat, don't go in the kid-chen." And if you're looking for a nice, quiet, slightly unrecognizable place to go . . .

CHAPTER 13

Greece and Other
Spots on the Map

THERE'S A FAMOUS old vaudeville sketch in which the comic —complete with pot belly, chin whiskers and low German accent—bounces onto the stage, looks around knowingly and then confidently announces, "Dis mus' be der Place!"

It never was the place—at least, not the place that *he* wanted. But he stayed, anyway, had fun and left them laughing.

I get the same feeling every time I read one of the descriptions gathered for this chapter. The places that the kids are talking about aren't exactly the way I remember them, but I stay with them, anyway, and they leave me laughing. I'm sure you'll laugh, too.

Get set to travel—but bring your own compass. . . .

Russia is also sometimes called the Union of Soviet Socialist Republics. We must watch for it under this disguise.

151

Q. What country is famous for the manufacture of goblets?
A. Turkey.

※

Most of the Atlantic is somewhat below sea level.

※

Chile is a long skinny country caused that way by much poverty.

※

To have an earth you must first get your thunder roaring and your earthquakes shaking and your volcanos spouting. It is a noisy business to become an earth, but it is worth it.

※

The Pacific Ocean could be famous as a mountain if it was not upside down.

※

The equator is where everybody equals everybody else.

※

One of the largest Indian reservations in America is Indiana.

※

Status quo means the existing state. There are presently 50 status quos.

※

Q. What do rivers help people do?
A. Drown.

With the aid of the camel, man can travel over the Sahara
Desert. Why man wants to travel over it, only man's intel-
ligence can figure out.

Gnomes live in Alaska in a city of the same name.

The worse thing about latitudes and longitudes and equators is that they are only imaginary places. People should not have to fill up their heads with imaginary places. We should use all our mind's space for the real ones.

Parasites are residence of Paris.

The most southern point of the United States is 2½ inches from the equator.

In Holland, children put out their shoes and St. Nicholas feels them up with candy.

Q. Why is so much of the world covered with water?
A. Because so little of it is covered with land.

A pueblo is a house unless it is in Colorado where it is a city. They like to do things bigger.

Suburbs are things to come into the city from.

The chief export of England is fog.

Although we live in the 20th century, here in the western hemispher it is only 1963. The further west we go the earlier it gets.

South is straight down, but don't go too far.

Contrary to popular opinion, Arizona is actually rather cold all year except from March through December.

Children do not have mothers in Spain, but they use madres to take their place.

The international date line is where people can go to make dates with those of a foreign sex.

Scientists say Alaska is getting warmer, but they're talking from California.

The sun gets to the Central Time Zone before the Mountain Time Zone because it's easier to travel on flat land.

West is for sunsets. It is an important direction for sleeping.

Atlantis is world famous for being lost.

People used to think the world was flat and if you came to the edge you fell off into what? Nobody knew for sure. This is just one of the things we know today that they didn't know.

Everything moves slow in Ertia.

As far as longitude is concerned Greenwich in England is nothing.

As the earth slowly rotates, each place gets its turn being Noon.

They say New York New York twice because of its hugeness.

Australia is located in the Pacific Ocean. It is presently still floating.

Going halfway around the world you end up farther away than going all the way around it. I think this was caused by somebody unbeknowingstly breaking our earth's time barrier.

If you keep going straight ahead, some say you would end up where you started! This is why some people think the earth is round. Actually, it is round for a very different reason.

Naughtical miles tell how far it is to places we shouldn't go.

There are four hemispheres called Eastern, Western, Northern and Southern. "Hemisphere" means half the world. We are allowed to have four halves only because the world is larger than anything else on earth.

B.C. is a prehistoric province of Canada.

Chicago is on Central Time, New York is on Eastern Time, and the Atlantic Ocean is on Mara Time.

French policemen often disguise themselves as gendarmes.

Mobile is a fast moving city presently located in Alabama.

Sea level is where water won't tip to one side or another but sits level if left alone.

Russian spies like to hide behind ironed curtains.

Longitude is another name for meridian, except in Connecticut where nobody ever heard of Longitude.

The speed of a ship is given in Nots. Being in water, they can never be sure.

Peruse are people who live in Peru.

The axis is only a make-believe line, but the earth somehow manages to turn on it.

The Arctic Circle is actually an Arctic Line. Maybe it is so cold up there people can't see straight.

A narrow neck of land is sometimes called an Isthmus, which looks like it is spelled wrong but it isn't.

Mountains were pushed up by gasses inside the earth, and what we see now is what was left when the earth's stomach settled.

Q. What is the highest mountain peak in Germany?
A. The Gesundheit.

We send our old summers and winters down to South America which is why they are always a season behind.

Brunei is a small, rain-filled island. Its overpopulation of rain has shrunk it rather badly.

Newfoundland is capitaled by a gander.

Men had trouble finding the North Pole, but any husky dog could find it easy.

And now, in case you can't find your way out of this cartographer's nightmare, maybe a few lessons in arithmetic will help. Beginning with the Continental Divide? . . .

CHAPTER 14

Pythagoras and
Other Squares

THIS IS A subject in which I should be quite adept—but I'm not, and I don't understand why. After all, you might say that arithmetic has been very important to my approach to life: for years I ran around in *circles* trying to find myself; I've always tried to play it *square* with everyone; I'm in a business where if you don't figure out the *angles* for yourself you're out of the business; I *added* a lovely girl to my life; we *multiplied*; we've never had even a *short division*; the *pluses* have been many, and even the *minuses* we've taken in stride. I've even bought a few *sub tracts* in my time.

So, why do I have to add up a long column of figures at least three times?

I'll read along with you as the kids give a refresher course —or, knowing the merry, madcap mathematics that is in store for you, I think I should say "refreshing course."

Fingers ready? Let's begin with five and six. Or, stated another way. . . .

In algebra you use X when you don't know what you are talking about.

An inclined plane is one that may crash.

Tangents are found chiefly in Florida and California.

Sum is not like Some. It is like All, added together.

Radium may be found anywhere from the center of a circle to the outside.

A circumference runs around outside a circle trying to get in.

To postulate means to stand up straight while giving the answer.

Nonplus means minus.

The hypotenuse is a humane device for hanging hypotemusses.

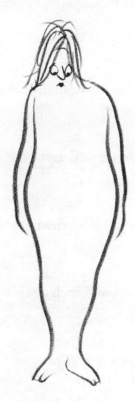

The perimeter is like the outer boundary of people with plain or ordinary figures.

Squares are circles with corners.

A rectangle is a sloppy square.

If you speak of a four-sided triangle you are speaking of either a rectangle or a square, depending on how it has its corners.

Vertical is the same as horizontal, only just the opposite.

Perpendicular is like vertical, but even more that way.

Furthermore is much farther than further.

Degrees tell us how round each circle is.

Here is a trickey question. What does ice and geometry have in common? Cube! Ha ha!

I thought out what a common denominator is twice, but I forgot it three times.

A circle is a surrounded nothing.

Minus means less that much while subtract means that much less.

Here is why 9 times 9 is 81. We all know that 9 times 10 is ninety. To keep this true, 9 times 9 has to be 81.

Equations are residents of the equator.

Q. What is the point of studying fractions?
A. The decimal point.

Q. If John lifts a box weighing 75 pounds to a height of five feet, how much work has he done?
A. He has hardly started to work.

Positive numbers are numbers written in ink.

Ten grams equal one epigram.

A quotient is when you say the words that somebody else said before.

Pythagoras is famous for noticing that triangles have three corners.

A pentagon is an eight-sided general.

The ozone is where the zeros are, like in 22,000 the ozone comes after the comma.

A rhombus is a dance in which you take equal steps to each side.

Right angles are 90 degrees. Left angles are right angles facing the other way.

When two things are parallel it means they are never cross to each other. But to make sure, they must never meet.

As I was saying at the beginning of the chapter—I should be quite adept in this subject, but. . . . Anyhow, I've learned enough to know we've come full circle, because we're right back to a kid's view of . . .

CHAPTER 15

American History — from the Alamo to the Carpetbeggers

Wᴇʟʟ, Mʀ. Lɪɴᴄᴏʟɴ was right: We *can't* escape History. The kids are about to do for our own country what they did for the entire world in Chapter One. I need not remind you that our country is a great one. We have lived through good times and bad; we have survived wars and depressions; we have taken the triumphs and the disasters in stride, and on the few occasions when we have gone off the deep end, our humor has given us back our perspective. We've survived, and we've grown. I mention this only because the country may be about to undergo its most severe test: The kids are ready to give their version of what happened, and how.

Well, as some unnamed hero of our past once said, if you can't be right you might as well be President. . . .

169

As soon as Columbus saw the Indians he immediately called them that. Somehow he knew that is what we would be calling them later on.

The War of Eighteen-Twelve was a war between America and England fought in 1776.

The Monroe Doctrine says no foreign doctoring is allowed here.

The Plain Indians were called that because they were plain, pretty homely in fact.

The bison roamed the great plains for many years under the name of buffalo. Despite this trick they were practically extincted.

America was found by four fathers.

A person who starts something is called a founder or trouble-maker.

Think of our ancestors. Are they behind us or did they go ahead of us? It is one of the mysteries of history.

The Japanese war lords called their army "invisible." Or maybe it was "invincible." Either way they couldn't be beaten. Later they were.

Before the time of George, Washington D.C. was A.C.

The pilgrims were very poor. They had to sail on a sunflower.

Posterity is the patriotic name for grandchildren.

The English, too, got many heros from the American Revolution. One of the greatest was Benedict Arnold.

It was hot on the open range of course. Many good foods were cooked there.

The causes of the Spanish-American War have a very short memory in my mind.

Wampum belts were worn by many Indians to hold up their wampums.

The Indians never thought of using wheels on a cart. They put their things in skinned bags and dragged them over the ground. That is what skinned them.

Upholstered is what a cowboy did just before he drew his gun.

The chief value of the War of 1812 was to help remember the date of.

The Revolution was caused because the English put taxis on our tea.

It is an act above and beyond the call of duty to have the Congressional Medal of Honor stuck in you.

1929 was experienced by the whole world.

The 2'nd world war was between the allies and the oxes.

When soldiers were bad and had to be punished they were sent to the whacks.

Abe Lincoln was broken hearted at the death of Ann Rutledge, but carried on with Ann Todd.

(*Ah, there, Mr. Lincoln, we really can't escape history, can we?*)

Soon after the Civil War, the South was invaded by a group of govt. men called Carpet Beggers. There was no income taxes then so the only way the govt. could make money was to sell used carpets.

A carpetbegger was a poor person who went around the south begging for it.

A president may be impeached if the charge is brought by Mister Meanor.

If neither the President or the Vice-President could serve, the next in line for the Presidency would be a temperate president.

Theodore Roosevelt was blind in one eye, but he could hear very well out of the other.

Q. How long did the Civil War last?
A. 22 pages.

Q. What was the immediate cause of World War II?
A. World War I.

So that they could not be stolen, the ranchers burned their initials on the cattle. It did not hurt like you might think because they were brandied first.

Q. Where did Thomas Jefferson live?
A. Thomas Jefferson lived in history.

Q. After his flight, where did Lindbergh come down?
A. Lindbergh went down in history.

※

Q. What did the explorers find in the interior of North America?
A. Lots of dirt.

※

The Puritans didn't believe in enjoyments or working on Sunday. I halfway agree with them.

※

The Hopi Indians got their name from a hopping dance they did.

※

Upon the invasion of Austria, America sent Hitler a scalding note.

※

The three people most influential in making Columbus' voyage possible were Nina, Pinta and Santa Maria.

※

The Quakers grew strong and famous for their breakfast food.

※

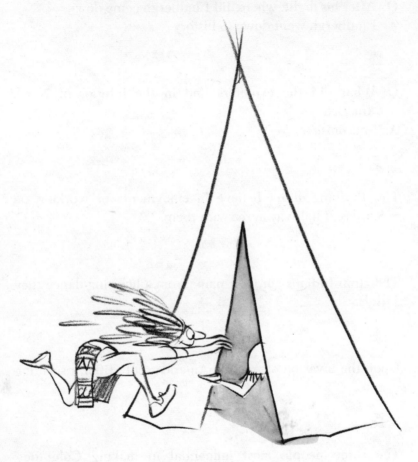

The Indians never smiled at the white man but they had a lot of fun in their teehees.

The most important qualification for a man who wants to be President of the United States is that he must be born.

Nathan Hale lost his life by dying.

The word "Hi" comes from the Indians, like in "Hi, Watha."

And now, stepping out of this bubbling stream of history, I see we have picked the Child's Garden of Misinformation *clean. Or is that a tiny blossom over there? It is, and a particularly appropriate one at that. Asked to describe her holiday, this wide-eyed wonder concluded:*

When we got home, we raped up the afternoon by attending a drive-in movie.

Alas, it is time we rapt up this book (or is it rapped?). It was, for me, the distillation of many, many hours spent in wandering the magic paths of childhood, guided—or charmingly misguided—by those wonderful creatures who live there. As long as there are kids, they will go on saying and writing the darndest things—and you and I will be privileged to share them.